AF228611

CRAYOLA

EDWIN BINNEY & C. HAROLD SMITH

Lee Slater

Big Buddy Books

An Imprint of Abdo Publishing
abdobooks.com

abdobooks.com

Published by Abdo Publishing, a division of ABDO, PO Box 398166, Minneapolis, Minnesota 55439.
Copyright © 2022 by Abdo Consulting Group, Inc. International copyrights reserved in all countries.
No part of this book may be reproduced in any form without written permission from the publisher.
Big Buddy Books™ is a trademark and logo of Abdo Publishing.

Printed in the United States of America, North Mankato, Minnesota
102021
012022

THIS BOOK CONTAINS
RECYCLED MATERIALS

Design: Emily O'Malley, Mighty Media, Inc.
Production: Mighty Media, Inc.
Editor: Liz Salzmann
Cover Photographs: Alexander Oganezov/Shutterstock Images (crayon box), Darryl Brooks/
    Shutterstock Images (crayons), Image provided courtesy of Crayola LLC and used with
    permission, © 2015 Crayola (Binney & Smith), rawf8/Shutterstock Images (paint), Vorobyeva/
    Shutterstock Images (clay clouds)
Interior Photographs: Andrea J Smith/Shutterstock Images, p. 7; Christopher Ziemnowicz/
    Wikimedia Commons, p. 17; Collier, John, Jr./Library of Congress, p. 9; Dan Cappellazzo/AP
    Images, p. 27; Ed Welter/Wikimedia Commons, pp. 13, 28 (top); Keith Homan/Shutterstock
    Images, pp. 23, 29 (bottom); Mighty Media, Inc., pp. 11, 28 (bottom right); RICK SMITH/AP
    Images, p. 15; Shutterstock Images, pp. 19, 29 (top); STEVE KLAVER/AP Images, p. 25; 365 Focus
    Photography/Shutterstock Images, p. 21; Wikimedia Commons, pp. 5, 28 (bottom left)

Library of Congress Control Number: 2021942804

Publisher's Cataloging-in-Publication Data
Names: Slater, Lee, author.
Title: Crayola: Edwin Binney & C. Harold Smith / by Lee Slater
Description: Minneapolis, Minnesota : Abdo Publishing, 2022 | Series: Toy stories | Includes online
    resources and index.
Identifiers: ISBN 9781532197093 (lib. bdg.) | ISBN 9781098219222 (ebook)
Subjects: LCSH: Binney, Edwin--Juvenile literature. | Smith, C. Harold, 1860-1931--Juvenile literature.
    | Inventors--Juvenile literature. | Toys--Juvenile literature. | Crayola (Firm)--Juvenile literature. |
    Crayons--Juvenile literature.
Classification: DDC 338.47688--dc23

CONTENTS

CHAPTER 1

ALL IN THE FAMILY

Edwin Binney was born in 1866 in Peekskill, New York. His father, Joseph, owned Peekskill Chemical Works. It made **charcoal** and **lampblack**.

C. Harold Smith was born in 1860 in England. He was Binney's **cousin**. In 1878, Smith moved to the United States. Smith and Binney would later make the world more colorful.

Peekskill was one of the country's early industrial centers.

CHAPTER 2

BINNEY & SMITH

In 1880, Joseph moved Peekskill Chemical Works to New York City. Both Harold and Edwin worked there as salesmen.

The company added new products, including red paint and **carbon black**. Joseph retired in 1885. Harold and Edwin took over the company. They renamed it Binney & Smith.

Many farmers bought Peekskill Chemical Works' red paint for their barns.

CHAPTER 3

A NEW MARKET

Binney **developed** new products. One was a black marker made with **carbon black** and wax. The marker was used to label boxes and barrels.

Binney's wife, Alice, was a teacher. Her students used a lot of pencils. Binney made pencil lead using local slate. Schools around the country provided a large market for the pencils.

In 1900, Binney & Smith
moved to Easton,
Pennsylvania, where there
were more slate mines.

CHAPTER 4

A NEW CHALK

Smith traveled to schools selling pencils. Many teachers said that **chalk** created a lot of dust. In 1902, Binney & Smith produced the first dustless chalk, An-Du-Septic Blackboard Chalk.

Teachers also said that crayons were expensive because they came from **Europe**. So, Binney got to work **developing** crayons.

An-Du-Septic chalk
is still being made
and sold today.

CHAPTER 5

CRAYOLA CRAYONS

Binney & Smith's crayons came out in 1903. Alice suggested the name Crayola. It was a combination of two words. *Craie* is French for **chalk**. *Ola* comes from the word ***oleaginous***. Smith and Binney loved Alice's idea, so Crayola crayons were born!

The original Crayola crayon box had eight crayons. They were red, orange, yellow, green, blue, violet, brown, and black.

CHAPTER 6

MAKING CRAYONS

Crayola crayons are made with **paraffin** wax. Large kettles hold the wax. Workers add powdered **pigment** and other ingredients to each kettle.

The wax mixture is then poured into **molds**. The wax quickly cools and becomes solid. Machines put labels on the crayons. Finally, the crayons are put in boxes and prepared for shipping.

A machine helps workers sort and package the crayons.

CHAPTER 7

ON THE ROAD

In the early 1900s, automobiles started being made in the United States. Car manufacturers had to purchase rubber tires for their cars. The strongest tires were made with carbon.

Binney & Smith had been making carbon for years. The company sold a lot of carbon to tire manufacturers such as the B.F. Goodrich Company.

In 1911, the B.F. Goodrich Company ordered 1 million pounds (453,592 kg) of carbon from Binney & Smith!

CHAPTER 8

GOOD PARTNERS

Binney and Smith worked well together. Smith was an excellent salesman. And he was good at **identifying** products people needed.

Binney was good at **developing** the products Smith suggested. He worked with the team at the factory. Binney and Smith's success was the product of a great partnership.

Nearly 3 billion Crayola crayons
are made each year.

CHAPTER 9

GIVING BACK

Binney and Smith became wealthy. To give back, Binney **donated** land and money for a park in Old Greenwich, Connecticut, near his family.

Binney & Smith also gave back. During the **Great Depression**, the company hired jobless local farmers to put labels on crayons. The community never forgot this **generosity**.

In the 1920s, Binney Park covered 10 acres (4 ha). It has since been enlarged to more than 30 acres (12 ha).

CRAYOLA CONTINUES

Smith died in 1931. Binney died three years later. Binney and Smith's company continued to grow without them. In 1998, Crayola crayons entered the National Toy Hall of Fame. To this day, Crayola delights **consumers** with its many fun products.

Today's Crayola products include crayons, markers, colored pencils, and more.
10 Classic Colors
Fine Line
Crayola
Long-Lasting, Brilliant Colors
Preferred by Teachers!
MARKERS
10
Nontoxic
10 Assorted Colors
Broad Line
Crayola
Preferred by Teachers!
MARKERS
10
Nontoxic
Crayola
Bright, Intense Colors!
COLORED PENCILS
64
Nontoxic
12
Easy Erase!
Crayola
Erasable
Colored Pencils
BUILT-IN ERASERS!
Non-Toxic
24
Bright and Vivid Colors!
Crayola
Preferred by Teachers
24
CRAYONS

CHAPTER 11

A CLASSIC TOY

Kids have been drawing with Binney & Smith Crayola crayons for more than 100 years. Your great-grandparents probably used Binney & Smith crayons!

Today, Crayola crayons are used by kids all over the world. The labels and boxes are printed in many different languages.

Hallmark Cards bought Binney & Smith in 1984. The company's name changed to Crayola in 2007.
Crayola
A HALLMARK COMPANY
LANE
25

CHAPTER 12

GOING GREEN

Crayola is committed to helping the **environment**. The Crayola Solar Farm uses **solar energy** to make electricity for the factory.

Today's Crayola is probably different than what Binney and Smith imagined. But both would be proud to see what their company has become.

The Crayola ColorCycle program turns recycled markers into fuel!
Crayola
COLORCYCLE iT!

TIMELINE

1860

C. Harold Smith is born in England.

1885

Smith and Binney take over Peekskill Chemical Works from Binney's father. They change the name to Binney & Smith.

1903

Binney & Smith produces the first box of Crayola crayons.

1866

Edwin Binney is born in Peekskill, New York.

1902

Binney & Smith produces the first dustless school chalk.

1931

C. Harold Smith dies.

1934

Edwin Binney dies.

1998

Crayola crayons are inducted into the National Toy Hall of Fame.

2007

The name Binney & Smith is officially changed to Crayola.

GLOSSARY

carbon black—a very dark black substance made mainly of carbon and used in products such as paint and shoe polish.

chalk—a stick made of soft rock used to write on blackboards and sidewalks.

charcoal—a black material that is a form of carbon.

consumer—someone who buys or uses a product.

cousin—the child of your aunt or uncle.

develop—to create something over time.

donate—to give.

environment—nature and everything in it, such as the land, sea, and air.

Europe—the continent between Asia and the Atlantic Ocean. England, Germany, and Italy are some of the countries in Europe.

generosity—the willingness to give or to share.

Great Depression—the period from 1929 to 1942 of worldwide economic trouble. There was little buying or selling, and many people could not find work.

identify—to find out what something is.

lampblack—black soot used to color things black.

mold—a hollow form in which something is shaped.

oleaginous (oh-lee-AH-juh-nuhs)—containing or producing oil.

paraffin—a type of wax often used in candles, drugs, and cosmetics.

pigment—a powder that is mixed with a liquid to create a color.

solar energy—energy from the sun that can be used for heating and generating electricity.

INDEX